In This Great Land of Freedom: The Japanese Pioneers of Oregon

Poetry by Lawson Fusao Inada
Historical essay by Eiichiro Azuma
Edited by Akemi Kikumura
      Lawson Fusao Inada
      Mary Worthington

Japanese American National Museum
Los Angeles, California

The catalogue for the exhibition *In This Great Land of Freedom: The Japanese Pioneers of Oregon* was funded in part by a grant from the M.J. Murdock Charitable Trust.

Book design: Joseph Erceg Graphic Design, Inc.

Library of Congress Catalog Card Number: 93-079005
Poetry written by Lawson Inada and historical essay by Eiichiro Azuma
Edited by Akemi Kikumura, Lawson Inada and Mary Worthington (Editors)
In This Great Land of Freedom: The Japanese Pioneers of Oregon
ISBN 1-881161-01-3

First Edition

Japanese American National Museum
369 East First Street
Los Angeles, California 90012-3901

Cover:
Suma and Teruo Tsuboi Family.
Ted (baby) and Akiko (sitting on wall)
Multnomah Falls, Oregon, 1917
Courtesy of R. Rowe

Printed in the United States of America

PREFACE

*O*ur task was to put together an exhibit telling the story of the "Issei Pioneers of Oregon," a story that spanned the years from 1885 through 1952. Could we do it?

At first, it seemed as though the project would be almost impossible to complete successfully. Although we expected grants in excess of $100,000, we would need to raise at least $30,000 from the local community. We felt that exhibit items, photographs, and documents would be difficult to find. Since the evacuation of 1942, most families had moved several times and with each move items had been lost. By 1993, the number of Issei had dwindled to only a few dozen and many were in poor health. With each Issei death, old photographs and documents, especially those diaries and letters written in Japanese, were discarded and lost forever. Finally, we wondered if we could locate any information about the earliest immigrants and their families.

Initial attempts by the Collections Committee to collect and identify old photos, documents, and other items confirmed our fears. The almost universal response from potential donors was, "I'm sorry, but we don't have anything of importance." The Campaign Committee's early efforts to raise $30,000 from the relatively small Japanese American community were slow to bear fruit.

As we continued making inquiries into the community, we let it be known that this was a last ditch effort to preserve the story of our parents and grandparents…a story that was fast disappearing. Fortunately, after a slow start, we located what turned out to be an important source of photos, historical items, and oral histories. These finds helped to generate enthusiasm and motivation. Soon donors began to realize that the small yellowing photo with worn corners of "Ma and Pa dressed in their shabby clothes or their funny looking suits and dresses" might tell a small part of the Issei story. The momentum increased when it was learned that the woman in an old church picture was the first Issei to settle permanently in Oregon. Goosebumps were felt when we discovered that people in the community had known members of the first Japanese family in Oregon. Photos emerged along with stories and letters. Soon we had a collection of over 700 photos and other articles for display. As word of the project continued to spread, we began hearing from former Oregon residents who had settled elsewhere following the war. Along with items for the exhibit, we were told stories that included the comedy, tragedy and intrigue that were integral parts of the Issei story. These were shared, sometimes discreetly, as enthusiasm for our effort grew.

The design and construction of the exhibit required considerable expertise. Watching these phases take form was an education in itself and comprise a separate story. Of course, this exhibit would not have started without the initiative and leadership of the Japanese American National Museum. The manpower within the state was inexperienced. Without guidance from the Museum we could not have put together this exhibition. Grassroots efforts by the Collection and Campaign Committees exceeded their initial expectations. We are indebted to the exhibition designers who contributed countless hours and great amounts of material to the project. Also, we express appreciation to the craftsmen, artists, photographer, docents and many others who volunteered their time, talents, and resources to round out the exhibit.

Naturally, our greatest salute goes out to the Oregon Issei who pioneered the way for all succeeding generations of Japanese Americans. Today, we enjoy more comfortable lives and have more opportunities than were available to them. Fortunately, we were able to preserve enough of the Oregon Issei story before it became a mere footnote in Oregon history.

George Katagiri
Project Coordinator
Portland, Oregon
June 2, 1993

INTRODUCTION

I. *H*ere is a picture of an Issei woman. What do you suppose she is thinking and feeling? Obviously, she is thinking about her grandson, and feeling joy, and love. She is also feeling the warmth of the sun, while enjoying a rare day off from her labors on the farm.

She can look back at her life with pride and satisfaction. Born and raised in a Japanese village, she came to America in 1901, joining her husband who had labored there since 1896. They became sharecroppers, moving from farm to farm with other pioneer families, making history and communities along the way.

Hers was a grueling, fulfilling life, full of struggle, sacrifice, celebration and wonder. She served as fieldhand, healer, community counselor, always counted on to hold things together. She could make soup from rain, beauty from scrap; she made everything feel special with her appreciation and grace. The land was beautiful, the harvests plentiful. What more to ask?

Thus, today, she feels happy, blessed. Within a year, she would be dead – and her grandson, Lawson, in a concentration camp.

II. *T*he Issei were a remarkable people…real American pioneers. Their journey, their quest, took them to a truly foreign country. The challenges were many. No Statue of Liberty welcomed them ashore. Instead, they were met with hostility and racism, with decades of discrimination in store.

The Issei were a determined people – determined to establish their place in this land of opportunity and promise. The odds were against them. That these "aliens" persevered and succeeded is a testament to their many strengths – of conviction, cooperation, organization, tradition. They were an industrious, resourceful people with a vision – and they did not lose sight of it.

Through all the hardships, obstacles, setbacks, the Issei remained a people of dignity and integrity, a people of goodwill, generosity, and respect for humanity. Through it all, they retained their faith in the American way. Theirs is a story of courage, the power of the human spirit, the love of life. Their legacy is for all to appreciate – "in this great land of freedom."

III. *C*ome, let us embark on this journey, this grand adventure known as the Issei experience. Imagine yourself in Japan, where you have lived all your life with your family. This is the home you love, the life you know – a difficult life, with little chance of improvement.

So when you heard about a strange and distant land called "America," you began to dream about moving there, to start anew. But it seemed like such an impossible dream, with too many risks and complications. After all, you couldn't just leave everything behind, taking your life in your hands…

Now you have your passage to destiny. Your hopes are high, but deep in your heart the doubts and fears arise. The whistle sounds. The ship is ready to depart. It's now or never. "Sayonara!" "Sayonara!" – perhaps forever.

The engines churn; your heart churns. There's no turning back. Already, your homeland shrinks in the distance behind you. You must turn your eyes to what awaits you – in "America" – across this great ocean of immeasurable size…

Birds call out, flying by. You look at your hands. You pray to succeed – and survive…

Lawson Fusao Inada
Ashland, Oregon
June 4, 1992

*Out there, somewhere,
is a place for me.*

Issei immigrants traveling
by ship to America
Location unknown, ca. 1907
Courtesy of Tamura Family

THE HISTORY OF THE ISSEI PIONEERS IN OREGON, 1880-1952

◆

*B*etween 1843 and 1860, more than 250,000 pioneers began the journey across the Oregon Trail heading west. In 1859, Oregon became one of the United States and was still a young state with undeveloped forests and virgin farmlands when the Japanese immigrants arrived in the 1880s. Called Issei, the first generation, Japanese immigrants, like all pioneers, struggled to survive in their new environment. Unlike most other immigrants, the Issei were classified as "aliens ineligible to citizenship" under American naturalization laws. They had to combat social and legal discrimination while they worked to create farms, businesses and communities for themselves and their children. Until today, the history of this courageous racial minority has been largely ignored.[1] Using primarily Japanese-language sources, this essay uncovers some of the forgotten history of the Oregon Issei and narrates their experiences as "aliens ineligible to citizenship" from 1880 to 1952.

THE ISSEI ARRIVE IN OREGON

◆

*Huge dreams of fortune
Go with me to foreign lands
Across the ocean.*

Rizan[2]

*A*merica beckoned to the adventurous and the industrious, first from Europe and then from all parts of the world. While European nations were claiming worldwide colonies, America's Commodore Perry sailed into

The first Issei Oregonian
Miyo Iwakoshi (center) with
brother, Riki, and adopted
11-year old daughter,
Tama Jewel Nitobe
Portland, Oregon, ca. 1886
Courtesy of G. Nomura

Underneath,
I am the
same person.

Railroad Camp, Mosaburo Matsushima (sitting center)
Location unknown, ca. 1895
Courtesy of Y. Matsushima

Last night, I dreamed I was home.

Tokyo Bay in 1853 ending two centuries of isolation. Perry's intrusion hastened the overthrow of the decaying feudal system and ushered in the Meiji Restoration of 1868.

Japan's new leaders embarked on a path of modernization transforming Japan into an international power. The small farmers bore much of the cost of change, which was accompanied by drought, famine and overpopulation. In the face of overwhelming pressures, the Japanese government finally allowed its citizens to work overseas.

The first known Japanese immigrants to

Oregon, Miyo Iwakoshi and her family, arrived in Oregon in 1880. Miyo's husband, Andrew McKinnon, was a Scot whom she had met when he worked as a professor of animal husbandry in northern Japan. They were accompanied to Oregon by Miyo's younger brother, Riki, and her adopted daughter, Tama Jewel Nitobe. The family settled near Gresham and established a sawmill which McKinnon named "Orient" in honor of his wife.[3]

Five years later, in 1885, Shintaro Takaki came to Portland to sell Japanese goods to

Chinese merchants. By 1889, he had accumulated enough money to start a restaurant. Two years later, he married Tama Jewel Nitobe, starting the first Japanese immigrant family in Oregon.

In 1891, a group of recently arrived Japanese gathered at Takaki's restaurant. They had discovered that the railroad jobs they had been promised were nonexistent. Generously, Takaki fed them on credit and found them work on farms and railroads.[4]

In a letter to a friend, Takaki explained:
In 1891, the first group of seven immi-

Wagon with wood pulled by four horses, men,
women in hats, and baby on chair
Nehalem, Oregon, ca. 1890s
Courtesy of G. Nomura

Our voices echo through the forest.

What will happen to my plans?

Shinzaburo Ban (1854-1931) was one of the largest labor contractors
in the Pacific Northwest. He supplied more than 3,000 Japanese
laborers a year for railroads and farms.
Courtesy of Oregon Historical Society (ORHI 48918)

grants, all from Okayama Prefecture, came directly to Portland under the contract that they pay back the travel expenses by working, followed by another group of thirteen from Wakayama Prefecture. Yet, they had great difficulty in finding a job. It was not until that fall that they could remit $20 per person to Japan which they earned at the hop farm in Sherwood. These 20 people were then taken by a man named Tadashichi Tanaka to Nampa, Idaho, to work on [a] railroad under a Chinese contractor.[5]

Tanaka, who would become the most influential labor contractor in the 1890s, asked

Takaki for more Japanese laborers to work on the Oregon Short Line, a subsidiary of the Union Pacific.[6] Takaki provided the workers and became the first Japanese labor contractor in Oregon.

By the turn of the century, the railroads had become a major source of employment for Japanese immigrants in Oregon. The labor shortage caused by the Chinese Exclusion Act of 1882 created a seller's market. In the 1890s, Japanese section hands earned $1.00 to $1.10 a day, while farm laborers received only 40 cents to 50 cents.

The number of Japanese railroad workers increased quickly from 600 in 1896 to 1,221 by 1906. Between 1905 and 1907, the Japanese comprised about 40 percent of the total railroad labor force in Oregon.[7]

Acting as middlemen between railroads and immigrants, labor contractors not only facilitated Japanese employment on the railroads but also made a large profit for themselves. Though the contractors received no compensation from railroad companies, each laborer paid a monthly total of $4.00 to his contractor. Each laborer was charged $1.00 a

Three Issei lumberjacks at Winans Lumber Camp
Dee, Oregon, ca. 1908
Courtesy of A. Dean

Roy Fukuda
Salem, Oregon, ca. 1900
Courtesy of F. Fukuda

With these hands
I earn my pay.

So quiet, calm. Outside, confusion.

month as a "translation fee," five cents a day for medical insurance and five cents daily commission. A Japanese railroad worker earned about $1.40 a day, or $35.00 a month in 1909, so more than ten percent of his entire income went to a labor contractor. Labor contractors also profited by selling their laborers daily necessities. Isolated in rural areas, Japanese laborers had no choice but to buy the over-priced goods provided by labor contractors. Many labor contractors used these profits to expand their businesses to larger ventures.[8]

Shinzaburo Ban was the most influential labor contractor in Oregon. Born in Tokyo in 1854, he was a son of a prominent *samurai* family and studied English under an American professor. After graduating from school, Ban started his diplomatic career, serving as a secretary to the Japanese Consul-General in Honolulu. There, he realized that labor contracting in the continental United States would lead to business opportunities. He resigned from the Japanese Foreign Ministry, set up an emigration company in Kobe and came to Portland in 1891. Taking

over the connections of Shintaro Takaki, Ban started out as a subcontractor for an American businessman, and in 1893, he established his own company known as S. Ban & Company. At one point, Ban had contracts to supply Japanese laborers to six railroad companies whose jurisdictions ranged from the West Coast to Nebraska and to North and South Dakota.[9] Concurrent with the massive influx of new Japanese immigrants from Hawaii and Japan in the early 1900s, his business prospered to the extent that he supplied 3,800 laborers annually for railroads and

Mother is always in my prayers.

First Congregation of the Japanese
Methodist Episcopal Mission
Portland, Oregon, 1903
Courtesy of Epworth United Methodist Church

farms and earned five million dollars a year. Also, he ran a large mercantile shop in Portland with branches in Denver, Colorado, and Sheridan, Wyoming, two mills in Quincy and Linden, Oregon, and a cattle ranch and a sugar beet farm.[10] S. Ban & Company was the biggest Japanese business in Oregon until its bankruptcy in 1924.

Because of the presence of Japanese labor contracting, Portland became a major center for the distribution of Japanese railroad workers in the Pacific Northwest. Workers were also sent to the salmon canneries and sawmills of Oregon, Washington and Alaska. In 1909, Oregon's sawmills had some 200 Japanese workers. During the ensuing decade, many Japanese entered the expanding lumber industry, which offered more stable employment than railroad and cannery work. In the meantime, as the Chinese rapidly decreased in number, more and more Japanese worked in the canneries. In the summer of 1909, for example, five hundred Japanese were sent from Portland to work in canneries. Many lumber and cannery workers were in Clatsop County, northwest of Portland. As late as 1920, there were 450 Japanese in the county, most of whom were laborers in the above two industries.[11]

In order to serve the needs of immigrant laborers, many ethnic businesses appeared in the Portland Japanese community. In general, Japanese businessmen were former laborers who successfully accumulated capital. During the first decade of this century, a number of businesses grew quickly along with the influx of Japanese immigrants into Oregon. By 1909, there was a total of 97 Japanese businesses, which included 14 western-style restaurants,

Shinjiro Sumoge (standing on log, far right)
and logging crew at Winans Lumber Camp
Dee, Oregon, ca. 1908
Courtesy of A. Dean

This tree was old as the Indians.

Tomorrow, more chopping, sawing.

A group of Issei men dressed in suits and a woman
dressed in western dress at Winans Lumber Camp,
(first row) Shinjiro Sumoge (second from left),
Takashi Inuzuka (fourth from left); (second row)
Tokuzo Takasumi (third from left)
Dee, Oregon, 1908
Courtesy of A. Dean

13 bath houses, 12 hotels and boardinghouses, 11 Japanese restaurants, 10 barber shops and 8 grocery stores.[12] Meanwhile, the Portland Japanese population also jumped from 20 in 1890 to 1,189 in 1900, and to 1,461 in 1910.[13]

EARLY JAPANESE LIFE IN OREGON

◆

*Working as a hop picker
It is impossible to
Return to Japan.*
Honda Fugetsu[14]

*B*efore 1910, the majority of the Oregon Japanese population were male laborers who lived in a crude environment. Initially, most, if not all, of them came to America not to settle, but to work and make money for their families in Japan. For these people, Portland was a temporary home to which they returned when they completed seasonal work. Until they found their next jobs, they stayed at Japanese hotels and ate at inexpensive restaurants. When the economy was unfavorable, these migratory laborers were the first to suffer. In 1907, a Japanese student described the tragic life of his fellow immigrants in these words:

Everywhere in the nation, the recession hit hard…. Railroad companies are firing laborers, and the daily wages dropped sharply from $1.45 to $1.10 and to $0.95….

This pain shall always remain.

Funeral of Mr. Yojiro Takeuchi's offspring
Hood River, Oregon, ca. 1906
Courtesy of Hiro Takeuchi

Mr. and Mrs. Yojiro Takeuchi and
children, Chiyoko and Thomas
Portland, Oregon, ca. 1909
Courtesy of H. Takeuchi

*These children
must speak English.*

In the downtown [Portland], Japanese hotels are filled with the [unemployed] people who cannot afford to buy a regular meal. Most of them barely survive by eating a piece of bread and water everyday. It is really unbearable to see such a misery.[15]

In the rural areas, the living conditions of Japanese immigrant laborers were equally poor. Some railroad workers reportedly lived in caves! An immigrant newspaper reporter who traveled into Huntington, Oregon, gave a vivid account of these cave homes:

To my surprise, I saw there was some-body watching us with just his head sticking up above the ground. I realized it was a cave he had there. The man invited us, "Come in," so we went down three or four mud steps. The inside was bigger than I expected. There, two Japanese about thirty years old looked at me and expressed their welcome, smiling. The cave was 16' or 17' square and about 7' or 8' high. On the ceiling – in other words, on the ground – they had put boards with canvas stretched over them, and on top of that, hay. They had two bunk beds.[16]

Others slept in tents or freight cars. Their daily meals were meager. In the early years,

railroad workers generally ate flour-dumpling soup known as *dango-jiru* with bacon, vege-tables and occasionally bread. Probably wary of white people who regarded Japanese as "unassimilable," labor contractor Tadashichi Tanaka required his workers to have "western-style" meals like Americans and not to use *miso* [Japanese soup base], soy sauce or rice. Ironically, the result of this "Americanization" in diet was harmful to the laborers and many reportedly suffered from night-blindness because of poor nutrition.[17]

Gambling and prostitution flourished in

Yojiro Takeuchi Barber Shop at N.W. 4th and Davis
Portland, Oregon, 1910
Courtesy of H. Takeuchi

When in America, smell American.

To gain respect, give respect.

Dressed for Portland Rose Festival Parade.
Standing, right: Katsusaburo Tamura;
seated, right: Masuo Yasui.
Two men on left unidentified.
Portland, OR, 1907
Courtesy of Homer Yasui

the bachelor community. As early as 1891, a Japanese Consulate official found some 40 Japanese gamblers and pimps in Portland. He also reported the presence of 19 Japanese prostitutes in the city, many of whom had moved from Seattle and entered prostitution as wives of gamblers.[18] Seventeen years later, another Japanese diplomat investigated the Portland Japanese community and depicted it as "obscene" and "even worse than China-town." In his opinion, the living conditions of the immigrants showed "no progress."[19]

An old-timer gave a vivid picture of early Japanese life in Portland. In the Japanese section of town, he worked as a dish washer in a Japanese restaurant from five in the morning until after midnight. Serving a meal for a dime, the restaurant catered to the Issei laborers who patronized neighboring gambling houses and brothels. He observed that Japanese gamblers liked to play cards, roulette and *hanafuda* [Japanese card game]. Some people gambled away thousands of dollars, while others won as much in a matter of a night.[20] In the eyes of many immigrant laborers, gambling seemed a short cut to their

dream: returning home with money.

There were some immigrants who sought to rid the community of these vices. Starting from 1893, Reverend Sadakichi Kawabe, who established the Portland Japanese Methodist Church, launched a campaign to reform public morals among Japanese residents. Community leaders such as Shintaro Takaki and Shinzaburo Ban gave their support to the campaign.[21] Shozui Wakabayashi, who came to Portland in 1903 as the first resident Buddhist minister, also contributed to the welfare of the early Japanese community. He

*At least I know
his family...*

Exchange picture of Masa Suzuki
sent to prospective groom,
Shinjiro Sumoge
Japan, ca. 1911
Courtesy of A. Dean

Exchange picture of Shinjiro
Sumoge sent to prospective
bride Masa Suzuki
Hood River, Oregon, ca. 1911
Courtesy of A. Dean

*She will
see I am
somebody...*

found work for the young men and offered other services they needed. In addition to serving the spiritual and social needs of the city people, Wakabayashi also toured from loggers' camp to camp and stayed with the laborers to whom he recited the Buddhist teachings. By 1911, the Oregon Buddhist Church expanded from two rented rooms to a newly constructed building, and parishioners numbered approximately 570.[22]

DEVELOPMENT OF JAPANESE FARMING COMMUNITIES

◆

*The untouched ground of America
I began to hoe
This virgin soil.*

Honda Fugetsu[42]

*D*uring the 1900s, many Japanese immigrants moved into agricultural work. At first, the Issei were drawn by better wages to work on farms. In 1909, farm laborers represented more than a quarter of the total 3,873

Japanese in Oregon. Known as *buranke katsugi* [blanket carriers], they were seasonal migrants, carrying blankets with a few other daily necessities. Many of these men subsequently invested their earnings and rose above the class of common laborers to sharecroppers, leaseholders and farm owners. According to the Portland Japanese Consulate Report, the number of Japanese farmers jumped from 71 to 233 between 1907 and 1910.[24]

Japanese immigrant farmers tended to gather in restricted areas. Montavilla and Gresham-Troutdale were prominent among

I must remember to be grateful.

Shuichi and Tazu Fukumitsu in front
of railroad car in which they lived
Banks, Idaho, ca. 1911-1912
Courtesy of Y. Kawase

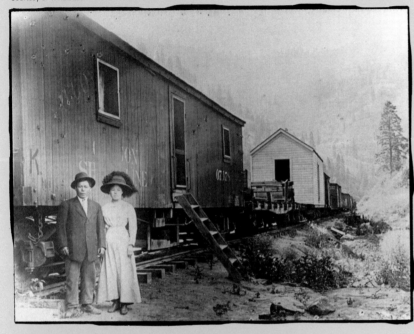

*Mosquitoes,
rain – I won't
complain.*

Takashi and Tomi Inuzuka
Independence, Oregon, ca. 1914
Courtesy of A. Dean

the many Japanese farm settlements in the eastern part of Multnomah County. Starting around 1904, Japanese emerged as berry and vegetable farmers in these areas. Land prices were high, from $500 to $800 per acre, so most Japanese were tenant farmers with three-to-six-year contracts. Initially, white landowners welcomed the Japanese on their land because they paid the highest rents, usually $15 an acre.[25]

Because of its close proximity to Portland, Montavilla was the first Japanese farming settlement with a sizable population. In 1908, 36 Japanese farmers held a total of 665 acres.[26] Three years later, the community had approximately 200 Japanese residents with an additional hundred laborers during the harvest seasons. Half of the total acreage in the area was under Japanese control by then.[27] The first Japanese producers' association in the state was established here. Montavilla was indeed, as a Japanese immigrant writer called it, "the Japanese farm village" at that time.[28]

The Japanese farming settlement expanded further east, and the Gresham-Troutdale area became its center. By 1920, local Japanese farmers were reported to have occupied half of the acreage of raspberries, 90 percent of the strawberries, 30 to 40 percent of the loganberries and 60 percent of all the vegetable and truck gardens. As did their Montavilla counterparts, the Gresham Japanese organized a farmers' association in 1918 in order to market crops and purchase equipment and supplies. The Gresham-Troutdale Farmers' Association had an initial membership of 50 farmers. In the eastern part of Multnomah County, there were almost 300 resident Japanese in 1920.[29]

Hood River, located some 60 miles east of

Postcard to Roy Fukuda from Y. Koda
Portland, Oregon, 1914
Courtesy of Frank Fukuda

*A strange way
to spend money.*

Portland along the Columbia River, was another major farm settlement for Japanese immigrants. The small valley was undeveloped until the turn of the century. When Japanese immigrants first came to the area around 1904, they were neither tenant farmers nor field hands. Many were employed to cut trees and to clear land by local landowners. They were given five acres in exchange for clearing 15 acres under a unique working arrangement with their employers. This arrangement enabled the immigrants to become landowners without accumulating capital.[30] By 1909, several Japanese owned five to ten acres by this method, and a dozen others were clearing land in order to acquire the acreage. In the years to come, Hood River became a very distinctive Japanese community in which most of the farmers were settled landowners.

Outside of Multnomah County, Hood River was the largest Japanese farming settlement. Many Japanese farmers appeared during the early 1910s. Between 1910 and 1913, the farming population in Hood River, Dee, and Parkdale rose from 12 to 53. Japanese land ownership went from 137 acres to 767 acres, while their leasehold increased from 73 acres to 105 acres.[31] Thereafter, the number of Japanese immigrant farmers did not increase as sharply, but their acreage continued to grow. In 1920, some 70 Japanese were reported to farm 2,050 acres, of which they owned 1,200 acres. As a result, the average Japanese farmer in Hood River held larger acreage than his counterpart in other locales.[32] This was indicative of the strength of the Issei farmers in Hood River.

Masuo Yasui played an important role in

This should show them back home.

Brides arriving from Japan
Location unknown, ca. 1920
Courtesy of R. Senda

I wonder how we have changed?

Hotel Ohio at S.W. Front and Madison Streets, operated
by Tomoichi Sumida and Mosaburo Matsushima
Portland, Oregon, ca. 1915
Courtesy of Y. Matsushima

the rapid development of this farming community. Born in Okayama Prefecture, he came to Seattle in 1902 at the age of sixteen to join his father and brothers, who were railroad workers. After going to Montana, he worked as a cook for a Japanese railroad gang. When he was eighteen, Yasui moved to Portland. After a few months, he found a position as a domestic worker with a white family and enrolled in night school. He learned English quickly and acquired a good command of the language. Working as a labor-contractor, he became an active leader of the Portland Japanese community.

In 1908, Masuo Yasui established the Yasui Brothers General Store in Hood River with his brother, Renichi Fujimoto. When he visited the small valley community the previous year, he was impressed by the beauty of the area and inspired by business opportunities he saw serving the increasing number of Japanese residents. Furthermore, the local Japanese led the sort of life that he himself believed in: permanent settlement in America. Shortly after his visit, Masuo Yasui wrote a thirty-page letter to his brother, Renichi, in which he stressed this belief:

> People always talk about "Going back to Japan as soon as possible." Should it really be the ultimate goal to live an idle life [in Japan] with American dollars?… I hope that you summon your wife and make a peaceful home in this great land of freedom. What is the use of going back to Japan and spending the rest of your life in that countryside?[33]

Yasui envisioned his store playing a pivotal role in the development of the Japanese permanent settlement in Hood River. Eventually, Renichi was persuaded to invest his savings in

Tsuboi family picnic. Children (left to right) Ted, Akiko, Hiroshi, Toshio; adults (left to right) Suma, Teruo, Masaichi, and unidentified
Portland, Oregon, ca. 1917
Courtesy of R. Rowe

Listen! Grandmother is calling!

Kazuo and Ishino Inukai at home
Dee, Oregon, 1917
Courtesy of R. Namba

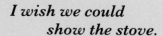

I wish we could show the stove.

a general merchandise store.

The store became the hub of community activities for the Japanese living in the Hood River Valley. As Masuo Yasui had envisioned its mission, the store was a meeting place, an information center, a rooming house, a mail drop and a travel and insurance agency for the convenience of local residents. Masuo, with his command of English, also served as a liaison between the Japanese and the local white residents, assisting the farmers in buying land and the laborers in finding employment. Opposing isolation from the white commun-

ity, he urged his fellow countrymen to spread out and mingle with their white neighbors.[34]

Masuo Yasui also moved into agriculture. His farming operation reflected his belief in permanent settlement in America. He purchased 320 acres of marginal land, which he offered to a dozen Japanese to cultivate. In exchange for their labor, these Japanese were given a part interest in the farms and orchards so that they could become landowners. Masuo also offered the settlers his financing and management skills.[35] Moreover, he showed his fellow Issei farmers the potential of such a

new crop as asparagus and inspired them to try their hands at it. With the leadership of Yasui, Japanese asparagus farmers later established the Mid-Columbia Vegetable Growers' Association which annually shipped 50,000 crates of asparagus to eastern markets. Masuo Yasui also produced large quantities of strawberries and other fruits. On the eve of World War II, ten percent of all the apples and pears in Hood River were shipped from his farms throughout the United States and to Europe. By that time, he owned a total of 880 acres in Hood River and 160 acres in Mosier.[36]

Sahei Watanabe and
Sadataro Yoshitomi farm
Milwaukie, Oregon, ca. 1917
Courtesy of M. Yoshitomi

Sometimes, I feel like the windmill.

Although few in number, Japanese immigrants also played a crucial role in the agricultural development of Lake Labish near Salem. In 1909, a former railroad worker, Roy Kinzaburo Fukuda, cleared 100 acres in the area to grow hops. Before long, he found the area most suitable for the production of celery and developed the famous Golden Plume Celery. By 1917, the dry lake was the exclusive settlement of Japanese farmers who cultivated between six acres to 20 acres each. Three years later, Lake Labish had some 30 farms with the population of 58 Japanese.[37]

Lake Labish Japanese farmers were well-known throughout the country for their superior celery. With Fukuda as the leader, they organized the Labish Meadow Celery Union. In 1925, the union shipped 314 freight cars, of which over 70 percent went to the eastern market. Interested in the fast growth of the farm community and its product, Senator Charles L. McNary of Oregon even paid a personal visit to Fukuda's farm. In appreciation, Fukuda sent a sample of celery to McNary and to President Coolidge.[38] In response, the Senator wrote, "I distributed it

among several of my senatorial friends, all of whom pronounced it the most delicious they [have] ever eaten…. I took a genuine pride in their commendation."[39] He added that the President also praised the celery. In the 1930s, the growers association increased its shipment to 700 carloads a year.[40]

American, Japanese – school is school.

Mrs. Goto driving an Oldsmobile
Russellville, Oregon, ca. 1917
Courtesy of G. Shido

*Driving is easy,
compared to work.*

Montavilla Japanese Language School,
teacher Mr. Nakano (center),
Kemy Hashimoto (front, third from right)
Montavilla, Oregon, 1918
Courtesy of G. Shido

JAPANESE IMMIGRANT FAMILIES AND COMMUNITY DEVELOPMENT

*"Japan is such a small island country
....What is the use of returning to
such a place? If we have to fulfill our
filial duty to parents and live with
wives, why don't we have them come
to America? If the difference in the
language and customs bothers us, why
don't we learn to adapt to them?"* [42]

Masuo Yasui [41]

*T*he rapid development of Japanese farm communities in Oregon was marked by the emergence of families. The early Japanese immigrant society was primarily a world of young bachelors. During the 1910s, the migratory nature of the community changed as more and more immigrants established their own families. As an unexpected consequence of the 1907-1908 Gentlemen's Agreement between Japan and the United States, there was a massive influx of Japanese women, including "picture brides." [42] Between 1910 and 1920, the Japanese female population in

Oregon rose approximately fivefold from 294 to 1,349. The newly-established couples were the foundation of Japanese farming settlements. In Hood River, for instance, most of the Issei farmers were married by 1920, making the male-female ratio four-to-three in the community. [43]

The Japanese immigrant family in Oregon was a microcosm of new sociocultural forms that emerged in the process of Japanese adaptation to Oregon society. Like other immigrants, the Issei brought their culture and traditions from Japan, but upon settling

To be a mother – such responsibility.

Mrs. Yoshi Kida (standing), Satsuki Azumano, George Azumano (child)
Portland, Oregon, ca. 1919
Courtesy of G. Azumano

Hold still now! Don't get dirty!

Tsukamoto and Nakamura Laundry
Salem, Oregon, ca. 1919
Courtesy of C. Donahe

in Oregon they began to adapt to the new environment. Some cultural elements were discarded while others were reinterpreted and renegotiated in response to the changing realities of life in America and the changing definition of what it meant to be a Japanese in Oregon.

One new sociocultural form was evident in the changing definition of gender roles in Japanese immigrant families. In Oregon, the Issei wives played multiple roles, breaking out of the confinement of traditional subordination. Not only did they take charge of domestic chores and child rearing, but they also played an indispensable part in the family economy. An Issei woman recalled those days:

Helping my husband, I worked so hard that I was amazed at myself. If we did not work hard, we couldn't go on living. When my husband failed in his business, I worked all the harder in order to help him start again. I drove a car around all over in order to buy several hundred dollars' worth of farm tools.[44]

An Issei man also described the hard work of the women with admiration:

When harvest season began, housewives got up at 5 a.m., fixed breakfast and looked after the horses. At 7 o'clock wives and husbands went to the orchards. They worked until 6 p.m. for twelve hours a day, except for one hour at lunch, day after day. Especially wives worked like plough horses, and even after dinner they worked with their husbands, boxing the fruit. Then after everyone else was in bed, they cleaned up and put things in order. For about a week every year they slept by their husbands in bed without even taking off their shoes, just cat-napping.[45]

Likewise, the men took on tasks that they would never have done in Japan. Since the

*I wish
this could
last forever.*

Rose Festival Parade, Oregon Japanese
Farmers' float made with vegetables
Portland, Oregon, ca. 1920
Courtesy of F. Fukuda

delivery of a baby cost $20 to $50, many Issei husbands acted as midwives for their wives. One man remembered how he had learned the necessary techniques of delivering babies from simple medical books. One veteran delivered as many as eight babies by himself.[46]

Mutual support was the new social norm on which Japanese immigrants built their families, communities and industries. Commercial and agricultural alliances, as well as individual diligence and persistence, were the best resources that the Issei had to achieve social and economic advancement in Oregon.

In Portland, Japanese merchants formed the Hotel Owners' Union, the Grocery Association, and the Laundry Union. Complying with the regulations and labor conditions set by the mainstream unions, these Japanese maintained good relations with the white business community, which promoted a favorable commercial environment in Portland.[47]

Issei farmers organized cooperative organizations which assumed a variety of roles ranging from supplying farm necessities to financing loans and from packing to collective marketing.[4] In the Portland vicinity, Hood

River, and Lake Labish, a number of Japanese growers' guilds were formed specializing in the production of cauliflower, green peas, strawberries, celery and asparagus. Based on mutual cooperation, Japanese farmers produced 90 percent of the state's cauliflower and broccoli, 75 percent of the celery, 60 percent of the green peas and 45 percent of the asparagus by 1941.[49]

Community institutions constituted another layer of sociocultural evolution in Japanese immigrant society. In order to meet the needs of the Issei, many organizations appeared

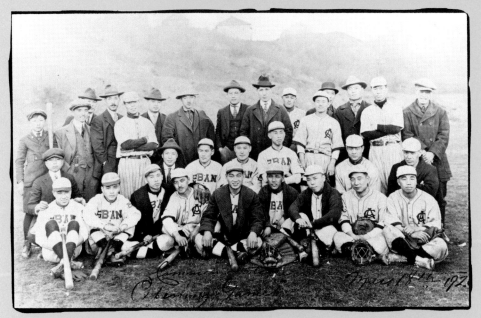

Commemorative opening game, S. Ban and CA teams
Portland, Oregon, March 18, 1920
Courtesy of L. Irinaga

To work as a team is important.

To play as a team is important.

Japanese Association, Daiichi Takeoka (first row, second from left),
Senichi Tomihiro (second row, second from left)
Portland, Oregon, ca. 1920
Courtesy of H. Yasui

within Japanese communities. They provided the residents with vital services ranging from administrative to religious and recreational to economic. First and most importantly, each Japanese settlement had a Japanese association.[50] The Japanese Association of Oregon in Portland functioned as a central organization, encompassing a number of local associations in Oregon, Idaho and Wyoming. In a sense, the network of local associations around this central body was the basis of community identity and solidarity among the Oregon Japanese. That network also enabled the asso-

ciations to become the community spokespersons, representing the best interests of the immigrants to the dominant society and even to the Japanese government.

The Japanese associations were crucial in the everyday life of the Issei. Under the Gentlemen's Agreement, if an immigrant wanted to re-enter the country and/or to summon his family members, he had to prove, with an official certificate issued by the Japanese Consulate, that he was a bona fide resident who had been in the United States prior to 1908. To obtain a certificate, the

immigrant applied to his local association. After checking the applicant's data, the association endorsed the application before the Japanese Consulate in Portland issued the appropriate certificate.[51] In the same way, local Japanese associations helped Issei men obtain the certificates they needed to defer Japanese military service every year.

Other community institutions included Japanese Christian churches, Buddhist churches/temples and prefectural associations. All these organizations helped the Oregon Japanese to adapt to the new envi-

Watanuki Family with friends
Parkdale, Oregon, ca. 1920
Courtesy of M. Yasui

*We cleared
     this forest in snow.*

ronment by satisfying their differing needs. Various cultural and sports groups, such as the *haiku* and *tanka* poetry societies and Japanese baseball leagues, added creative and recreational elements. Within the close knit community, they also had their own newspaper. Established in 1904, the *Oshu Nippo* was a prime source of information for both Portland residents and those in outlying areas of Oregon and Idaho. Although the Oregon Japanese were dispersed widely throughout the state, they were well informed of what was going on in their community.[52]

THE STRUGGLE AGAINST EXCLUSION

◆

*A series of exclusions
Now getting used to it
I spend each day farming.*
Honda Fugetsu[42]

*W*hile building their community and industries, Japanese immigrants struggled against exclusionists' threats. Combined with the rise of anti-foreign sentiments of World War I, the rapid growth of Issei agriculture stirred

whites' fear of Japanese competition. As the Hood River Japanese farmers showed a notable prosperity with a high level of land ownership, they became the prime target of organized exclusionist attacks. The local American Legion was the forerunner of the movement. It not only opposed Japanese land ownership in Hood River but also called for state and federal laws to strip them of legal rights in farming. In 1919, under the leadership of the Legion leaders, the Anti-Asiatic Association was organized, in which most of the prominent citizens of Hood River partici-

Relaxing after picking strawberries at the Sakuma farm
Parkdale, Oregon, ca. 1922
Courtesy of H. Saito

Ah, the sweet taste of celebration!

*Festive food!
Lanterns,
dancing!*

Yamada/Tanaka koto and shakuhachi concert
Portland, Oregon, 1924
Courtesy of R. Rowe

pated, pledging neither to sell nor to lease land to the Japanese. As the chief reasons for Japanese exclusion, the organization cited the rapid growth of Japanese land holdings, their economic threat to white farmers, high birthrate and low standards of living.[54]

Masuo Yasui stood up for his fellow Issei residents in Hood River. He first refuted the charge of Japanese "domination" by citing the fact that a total of 70 Japanese farmers controlled only two percent of all farmland in the Hood River Valley. Yasui also took issue with the Anti-Asiatic Association's figure of 800

Japanese in the county. Referring to the figures of the 1920 U.S. Census and Japanese Consulate Report,[55] he estimated the presence of 362 Japanese in Hood River, which was in fact a reduction of more than a hundred since 1910. The relatively high birthrate, he stated, was because most of the Issei had just started their families during the past decade. Lastly, he blamed white landowners for the low living standards of Japanese farmers, since they were the ones who provided the ill-equipped dwellings for the tenants.[56]

In an effort to better their community and

to make white Americans accept them as equally civilized people, Yasui also compiled a list of his "requests to Japanese ladies," which he probably distributed to other Issei.[57] After asking the women to "cultivate common sense," he argued, "You, the Japanese wives, are the 'diplomats' who represent all Japanese women, and you have greater influence than the Japanese government officials." Yasui then warned the Issei mothers not to leave their children unattended while working in the field. Rather than to make a fuss over money, he urged them to pay more attention to the

Oregon Buddhist Church at
N.W. 10th near Everett, honoring
Daika Sonyu Ohtani from Japan
Portland, Oregon, ca. 1925
Courtesy of J. Matsumoto

*Incense, the old
moonlit temple…*

care of children. In the end, he also added, "These are applicable not only to the women. I hope their husbands…will take the lead."

Hoping to settle the agitation once and for all, the Issei of Hood River entered into direct negotiation with the Anti-Asiatic Association. As their representative, Yasui delivered a proposal to stop voluntarily further Japanese land ownership and migration into Hood River in return for the cessation of the agitation.[58] After making that proposal, he contended that no one could blame his fellow residents for wishing to remain in the valley where they had

established their families and farms for years. In order to live in harmony with their white neighbors, the local Japanese were eager to enter any agreement based on fairness.[59] Nevertheless, the exclusionist group chose to seek discriminatory legislation against the Japanese rather than bring the local friction to an end.

During this period, anti-Japanese agitators succeeded in stopping the expansion of Japanese farming activities in other locales. Central Oregon was a case in point, in which even the powerful "Potato King," George

Shima, was forced to give up farming. In 1919, he and two white entrepreneurs purchased 13,800 acres near Redmond in the Deschutes Valley. He brought a handful of Japanese potato experts and field hands to raise the seeds for his California farms. This move upset the local white farmers as they saw "the acquisition of land by Japanese and the subsequent introduction of Japanese tenants and labor" as "detrimental to the best interests of the American farmer and businessman."[60] Forming the Deschutes County Farm Bureau, they stood against the project. Encountering

Mikasa Orchestra, Toru Kobayashi (second from left),
Mrs. Tateishi (only woman)
Portland, Oregon, ca. 1924
Courtesy of L. Irinaga

American jazz – the new tradition.

*Teacher says turkey
comes from Indians.*

Sadaji and Kikuo Shiogi Families
Portland, Oregon, ca. 1925
Courtesy of L. Sato

the county-wide opposition, Shima was forced to promise to neither introduce Japanese immigrants nor sell the land to them. Between 1922 and 1923, similar organized movements kept Japanese immigrants from settling in Prineville near Redmond, as well as in Medford near the California border.[61]

In the Oregon state legislature alien land bills were introduced in 1917, 1919, 1921 and 1923. The Anti-Asiatic Association, the Oregon American Legion, the Ku Klux Klan and opportunistic politicians were among the bills' major endorsers. Using the term "aliens ineli-gible to citizenship," the goal of these bills was to prohibit land ownership and leasehold by Japanese immigrants.[62] Since the majority of Japanese farmers, except in Hood River, were still tenants, the alien land law, if enacted, was likely to hinder their economic advancement.

Japanese immigrant leaders made every possible effort to prevent the enactment of the bills. They hired a white lawyer and sent him to the state legislature to lobby on their behalf. At the same time, they sought the support of the Portland Chamber of Commerce on the issue.[63] Having an economic stake in inter-national trade with Japan, the Portland bus-inessmen were eager to use their political influence on behalf of Japanese immigrants. Their involvement created enough support to kill the first three bills before enactment.

The Issei leaders believed that they would be vindicated if they continued their struggle against exclusion. Senichi Tomihiro, a Portland leader, wrote after the 1917 bill was shelved:

It seems unlikely that those anti-Japanese agitators suddenly will change their minds and that the issue will disappear. If an alien land bill is introduced every year, we have to

Judo instructors, (left to right) Frank Tomori,
Art Sasaki, Bun-Uyemon Nii (headmaster),
Senta Nii, Toru Kobayashi
Portland, Oregon, 1926
Courtesy of L. Irinaga

As in judo, as in life.

A fine future beckons the children.

The Yasui family, left to right: (children) Yuka (baby), Robert, Homer, Roku,
Michi, Minoru, Ray; (adults) Shidzuyo, Masuo, Renichi Fujimoto
Hood River, Oregon, ca. 1927
Courtesy of Yasui Family Collection

fight it to the death each and every time and protect our right to own land.... Hopefully, during that time, the "flowering spring" will come with a fundamental solution for the right of naturalization.[64]

Despite such a hope, however, between 1922 and 1925 the Oregon Issei encountered a series of oppressive statutes and practices by the federal and state governments, as well as violence from the exclusionists. In 1922, the United States Supreme Court ruled that a Japanese immigrant named Takao Ozawa was not eligible for citizenship because he was non-white.[65] With this decision, the United States officially established the legal status of the Issei as "aliens ineligible to citizenship," thereby making them virtual "second-class citizens." Two years later, based on this classification, Congress passed the Immigration Act of 1924 which prohibited the further entry of Japanese immigrants.

In 1923, the state of Oregon enacted two laws that discriminated against the Issei: the Alien Land Law and the Alien Business Restriction Law. The former legislation aimed to reduce Issei farmers to common laborers by prohibiting their land ownership and leasehold. The Alien Business Restriction Law attempted to destroy Japanese immigrant businesses. It allowed municipal governments to refuse business licenses to aliens for the operation of pawn shops, pool halls, dance halls or soft drink establishments. The law also required grocery stores and hotels run by aliens to display the signs of their nationalities, thereby enabling customers to choose which businesses to patronize on the basis of race and ethnicity.[66]

The final blow was the infamous Toledo

Go (Japanese board game) tournament
Portland, Oregon, ca. pre-World War II
Courtesy of H. Saito

金九碁囲市砕　念紀四一第

***Father was
champion
of the village.***

incident of 1925, in which Japanese sawmill laborers were violently driven out of the town by a mob of local whites.[67] Although the Issei eventually won a lawsuit against the mob leaders, this incident was a clear message of rejection from the white society. Denied naturalization rights in this country, the Issei were now subject to permanent legal discrimination. Such a grim reality caused the exodus of the Issei from Oregon, probably to Japan. Between 1924 and 1928, their population dropped from 2,374 to 1,568 in Oregon.[68] It represented more than a thirty percent decrease.

After the mid-1920s, the Issei's hope rested with their American-born children, the Nisei. Hood River farmer, Kohei Koana, spoke of it in a sarcastic way:

The Alien Land Law is now strangling us with its devilish hands. Even if such oppression gets eased in the future, we will probably be too old to work on farms by then…. Japanese farmers might disappear from Oregon within the next twenty years, unless the Nisei can successfully take over.[69]

By virtue of their citizenship, the Nisei had all the privileges and rights which were denied

to the first generation. Thus, despite the Alien Land Law or the Alien Business Restriction Law, the Issei could still lease or purchase farmland, as well as operate businesses, in the name of adult Nisei. On the eve of Pearl Harbor, for example, the Japanese farms in Oregon cultivated under the names of the Nisei constituted approximately 81.1 percent of the total.[70]

During the twenties and thirties, Japanese immigrants devoted themselves to building a firm economic and social foundation for the second generation. The Issei believed that the

Grocery store at 801 N.W. 23rd Street, (left to right) Jiro Sumida,
Shuichi Murakami (owner), Yamako Murakami
Portland, Oregon, ca. 1937
Courtesy of J. Murakami

If we don't have it, we can get it.

*I love
the feel
of the wheel.*

Hatsumi Nishimoto driving a tractor
Hood River, Oregon, ca. 1932
Courtesy of M. Yasui

future of the Nisei would be bright if they could succeed economically. To secure their agricultural foothold Issei farmers concentrated on the production of the crops that white farmers ignored.[71] Merchants also worked hard in order for their Nisei sons and daughters to get higher education. An Issei woman noted that she and her husband struggled to "send [their] children to college so that they wouldn't be inferior to Americans."[72] A hotel proprietor also said that he and his wife "kept working silently" despite the frequent insults by white customers because their

"earnest desire was to send [their] children to college by all means."[73]

By the late thirties, it seemed to the Issei that the Nisei were almost ready to become the successors to the Japanese community. In 1940, when the Portland Chapter of the Japanese American Citizens League (JACL) hosted the National Convention, the president of the Japanese Association of Oregon stated to the local Nisei as well as to the delegates from other communities:

We rejoice that the patience of the first generation is now receiving its reward; that

our hope is being fulfilled; that our faith is being justified and that our cherished desires have now been realized by the solid formation of your league, especially, your sincere efforts towards betterment of social, political and economic conditions. They are greatly appreciated.... I count upon you to contribute your share to the elevation of the high standard of American citizenship by broadening the traits which you have so proudly inherited from your parents.[74]

Nevertheless, the Issei's "hope," "faith" and "cherished desires" were all abruptly smashed on the fateful day of Pearl Harbor.

Community celebration at
Japanese Community Hall
Hood River, Oregon, ca. 1930
Courtesy of M. Yasui

United we stand –
Japanese Americans.

M. K. Farm Store owned by Masaichi Kanaya
at 212 S.W. Yamhill Street,
(left to right) Fumiko Kanaya, Jimmie Kanaya,
Meddy Itami, Ruby Kanaya, Masaichi Kanaya
Portland, Oregon, ca. 1928
Courtesy of R. Suzuki

I remember planting
all these things.

PEARL HARBOR: DAYS OF ANGUISH AND CONFUSION

We have spent two-thirds of our lives
in the United States and we feel we are
more American than Japanese; we are
willing to do anything we may be
asked to do to help our foster mother.
A Portland Issei, January 23, 1942[75]

Japan's attack on Pearl Harbor had a pro-
found impact on Issei life. Immediately classified as "enemy aliens," they were no longer
able to assure security for themselves or for
their children. "Asleep or awake, I felt as if I
were losing the color in my face," said a
Portland merchant. "I knew that our lives as
well as our property were at stake. I wondered
what would happen to us."[76] They faced a
difficult choice. On the one hand, Japan was
the country in which their parents, siblings
and friends lived. Moreover, denied naturalization rights in America, Japan was still their
country of citizenship. On the other hand,
America was their adopted country where
they had established their families. It was also
the country where their children and grand-
children would remain for the years to come.
A Hood River farmer recalls the anguish of
choosing one over the other: "We were all
terror-stricken at the news. War between
America, where we would live until death,
and Japan, where we came from! I am a
Japanese subject, but my children are Nisei,
and American citizens. We Issei were sorely
troubled by this war."[77]

Yet, the great majority of the Issei cooper-
ated with the war effort of the United States
from the beginning. Parents encouraged their

Japanese Community Church
Salem, Oregon, ca. 1938
Courtesy of F. Fukuda

SALEM, ORE
Sept 18th 1938   10th Anniversary Japanese Community Church.

*They always make
me feel welcome.*

sons and daughters to render service to their country in the time of crisis. For example, on the very day of the attack on Pearl Harbor, Masuo Yasui of Hood River sent a telegram to his son, Minoru, in Chicago, urging him to serve in the military.[78] Many Issei also contributed financially to the country. According to Yasukichi Iwasaki, when the government lifted the freeze on the Issei bank accounts, he immediately withdrew $425, spent $375 for U.S. Defense bonds and donated $25 to the Red Cross.[79]

The Issei publicly showed their support to the United States. On January 23, 1942, Portland residents held a mass meeting and sent President Roosevelt a telegram to affirm their loyalty: "We old Japanese pledge our services and our resources to destroy Japan and her Axis partners who challenge our democracy."[80] In Hood River, all the Issei signed a common pledge, which read:

Most of the alien Japanese residents are devoted to this great Democratic America although we are not eligible for citizenship. We love this country so much that we wish to live here permanently.... May we pledge

our loyalty to the Stars and Stripes just as do our children who are patriotic American citizens.[81]

Still the Issei were bewildered, confused, angry, frightened and helpless. The continuous fear of the unknown future, coupled with an upsurge of anti-Japanese sentiments, brought about an enormous emotional drain. Yasukichi Iwasaki repeatedly expressed such feelings in his diary. On December 13, he wrote, "The war is causing all sorts of worries among the Issei, and nobody can work. We all seem absent-minded."[82] Two weeks later, he

I never get tired of waving.

Japanese Association float in Rose Festival Parade, (left to right) Mary
Marumoto, Chiyo Minami, Yaeko Inuzuka, Nobuko Ochiai
Portland, Oregon, ca. 1939
Courtesy of M. Nakadate

Cookie's Grocery Store, Teruye Katagiri
(in foreground) with customers
Portland, Oregon, 1939
Courtesy of R. Senda

Our customers, our friends.

made a similar entry: "Ever since the war broke out, I've been feeling unpleasant. Being in the state of emptiness, I do not do anything. I do not have anything to write about."[83] At one point, the mounting sense of fear and helplessness caused Iwasaki to stop writing in his diary for two weeks, because he "lost courage to do so."[84]

The war suddenly stripped the Issei of autonomy over their life and community. On December 7, President Roosevelt issued an executive proclamation, under which their activities were greatly restricted. The local law enforcement authorities and the FBI destroyed the leadership of the Japanese community by rounding up Issei leaders and sending them to various Justice Department prison camps. This resulted in the dissolution of the Japanese associations and other organizations that had served to combat social and legal discrimination prior to 1941.

Under these circumstances, the Nisei began to assume new leadership in the community. Between December, 1941 and March, 1942, federal and local governments as well as military authorities issued a number of orders and proclamations. Given their limited English skills and their "enemy alien" status, the Issei turned to their children and to the JACL to interpret the orders and meet the requirements.[85] For instance, on behalf of his parents, a Nisei man wrote to the JACL to inquire about travel restrictions on the Issei. According to the letter, his family had farms in Boring and Sherwood. Both farms needed attention as winter passed into spring. In reply, the JACL secretary sent him applications for travel permits with procedural instructions.[86] On another occasion, when the city of

Issei and Nisei men pledging support of U.S. war effort, (left to right) Mr. Shioshi, J. Kida, unidentified, unidentified, Mr. Nakata, S. Shiogi, H. Azumano, Mr. Tanaka, N. Horagami, R. Koizumi, K. Nakayama
Portland, Oregon, 1941
Courtesy of L. Sato

With money, with sons – we pledge allegiance.

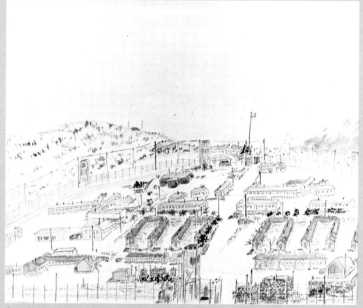

Santa Fe Alien Detention Center, sketched by Issei internee, artist unidentified
Santa Fe, New Mexico, ca. 1943
Courtesy of K. Takeoka

Is this why I came to America?

Portland denied the renewal of business licenses to Japanese immigrant merchants, the JACL acted as their agent and asked the governor to intervene, although it was in vain.[87] As the Issei saw it, the JACL was the only viable organization to represent the interests of the Japanese community.

Meanwhile, the pressure of mass "evacuation" became greater day by day. In the middle of February, various American Legion posts started to demand the removal of both the Issei and the Nisei from Oregon.[88] At the Congressional committee hearing held in

Portland, the Mayor of Portland and the delegates from Hood River warned that the presence of Japanese residents was a threat to national security. Anticipating the economic benefits of Japanese exclusion, the Hood River Apple Growers' Association openly stated that the white farmers were prepared and desirous of taking "over the [Japanese] properties and running them efficiently."[89]

The federal government was moving toward the mass exclusion of Japanese residents from the Pacific Coast states. On February 19, 1942, President Roosevelt signed

Executive Order 9066 which authorized the army to remove any individual from designated zones without due process of law. Less than two weeks later, John L. DeWitt, Commander of the Western Defense Command, issued Public Proclamation No. 1, which designated the western half of California, Washington, and Oregon as Military Area No. 1 and the rest of these states as Military Area No. 2. This proclamation also suggested that the Japanese might be excluded from Military Area No. 1.

The diary of Yasukichi Iwasaki illustrates

Issei internees at the Santa Fe Alien Detention
Center (mostly Issei leaders from Oregon)
Santa Fe, New Mexico, July 14, 1943
Courtesy of K. Takeoka

*Bluejays
fighting in
the pines.*

the confusion that the people went through after DeWitt's order.[90] For the first time on March 8, Iwasaki discussed the likelihood of "evacuation" with his sons. By the following day, they agreed to lease out their property during the period of evacuation and informed their lawyer of that decision. His son was to negotiate with the lawyer and a prospective lessor and to liquidate the family assets, while Iwasaki himself concentrated on the management of their 50-acre farm. However, as Iwasaki made his son prepare for evacuation, he also asked for loans from a local bank and

a cannery for the harvest of strawberries in the summer. This contradictory behavior reflected his mixed emotions. On the one hand, he had to accept the reality of evacuation, "no matter how unwilling he was."[91] On the other hand, he still could not believe that he would actually leave Hillsboro before the harvest.

Nonetheless, the answers that the bank and the cannery gave to Iwasaki forced him to realize the reality. The former refused any loan to the Japanese, whether there was collateral or not. The latter abruptly canceled

the verbal agreement which it had with Iwasaki for years. After these rejections, his diary was filled with expressions of futility and depression. On March 18, he wrote, "The thought of evacuation has just tormented me since morning. I cannot go about my work at all."[92] Four days later, he suggested that he had lost a sense of purpose in life. "I feel very dispirited. I just live to eat everyday. I will never forget this wasteful life."[93] In another entry, Iwasaki stated that the circumstances drove "us Japanese almost to distraction."[94] A few days later, Iwasaki concluded a lease

Soldiers assisting evacuees
Portland, Oregon, 1942
Courtesy of Oregon Historical Society (ORHI 49760)

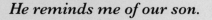

He reminds me of our son.

Junichi Doi checking in at
Portland Assembly Center
Portland, Oregon, ca. May, 1942
Courtesy of Oregon Historical
Society (ORHI 28162)

*19228
– remember
that number.*

contract with a white farmer. Many Issei, like Iwasaki, experienced indignation and dejection, since they, too, found their customers, associates and neighbors turning their backs on them.[95]

The forced evacuation of the Oregon Japanese and the American-born Nisei and Sansei took place in May, 1942. The Portland residents were the first to be uprooted from their community to an "assembly center," followed by those from Gresham, as well as Washington, Clackamas, Columbia and Clatsop Counties.[96] Four months later, 2,318

Oregon Japanese and Nisei were transported by train to the Minidoka "Relocation Center" in Idaho, while a few hundred were sent to the centers in Tule Lake, California, and in Heart Mountain, Wyoming.[97] The Japanese of Hood River and Marion Counties were not part of this group. They were taken to the assembly center in Pinedale, California, and then to Tule Lake.[98] When mass removal was completed, the Minidoka internment camp had 65.3 percent of the Oregon Issei and Nisei, Tule Lake 32.2 percent, and Heart Mountain the rest.[99]

ISSEI LIFE BEHIND BARBED WIRE

◆

*The harsh winds of autumn
Pierce the spirit of those
Who live at the mercy of fate
Created by the war.*

Akiyama[100]

*T*he internees had primitive living conditions. The North Portland Assembly Center had previously been used as the Pacific International Livestock Exposition Building

Waiting to register at the Portland Assembly Center
Portland, Oregon, ca. May, 1942
Courtesy of Oregon Historical Society (ORHI 49759)

At least we're still in Oregon.

It still smells like animals.

Hiroko Terakawa (left) and Lilian Hayashi
in Reverend T. Terakawa's cubicle
in Portland Assembly Center
North Portland, Oregon, May 31, 1942
Courtesy of Oregon Historical Society (ORHI 28163)

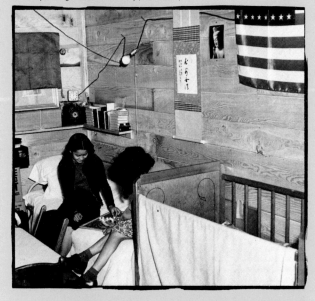

and was barely adapted for human habitation. Each family was assigned to a small, single room in a large barrack with walls made of thin plywood sheets. In order to make each room as "homey" as possible, the internees made shelves, tables, chairs, cupboards and other furniture and appliances for themselves. They hung curtains or put up screens to separate sleeping quarters between adults and children. Despite those efforts, privacy was non-existent. The sound from neighbors was heard continuously, and washing, toilet and shower facilities were shared by other residents of the barrack. They also ate their meals at mess halls.[101] These conditions remained much the same even after the people were moved to internment camps.

During their incarceration, the life of the Issei completely changed. The camp authorities provided meals and basic daily necessities, as well as some spending money. Consequently, the Issei were not required to work for subsistence, although many of them volunteered for skilled and unskilled employment for which they were paid minimal wages set by the government.[102] The wives' domestic duties included family laundry and room cleaning. Childcare took less time because, given the small living quarters, the children tended to spend their time outside, playing and eating with friends. This disrupted the close knit family life which characterized Japanese families, although it enabled the Issei to engage in various recreational activities ranging from English learning to creative arts.[103]

In February and March, 1943, the War Relocation Authority (WRA) conducted the "army enlistment and leave clearance regis-

At least we're still in America.

Leaving the Portland Assembly Center for an internment camp
Portland Union Station, August, 1942
Courtesy of Oregon Historical Society (CN 021090)

Minidoka internment camp, kitchen helpers, Block 30
Minidoka, Idaho, ca. 1943
Courtesy of Y. Morita

Old, young, everyone depends on us.

tration" in order to separate the "loyal" internees from the "disloyal" ones. In the questionnaire administered to the internees, question number 28 asked if they were willing to "forswear any form of allegiance or obedience to the Japanese emperor." From the Issei perspective, this question only reinforced the dilemma that had haunted them since Pearl Harbor. Because the Issei were "aliens ineligible to citizenship" in America, it virtually forced them to become persons without a country. Some were also afraid of the possible consequence of family separation, while others worried about the welfare and future of their children.[104] After considering all these factors unrelated to their "loyalty" to America, the vast majority of the Oregon Issei answered "yes" to this question.[105]

Through this questionnaire, the WRA also intended to recruit Nisei volunteers for the Army. Thousands of the Nisei from ten internment camps served in the military to vindicate not only themselves but also their parents. Along with the Nisei from Hawaii, they formed the 100th Battalion and the 442nd Regimental Combat Team and fought in the European theater, during which time they earned the distinction of being one of the most decorated combat units. In the Pacific theater, a few thousand Nisei served in the Military Intelligence Service, utilizing their Japanese language skills to interrogate captured enemy soldiers and translate documents. Among them was Sgt. Frank Hachiya of Hood River who received a Distinguished Service Cross for uncovering the Japanese defense lines in the Philippines at the cost of his own life.

Those clouds float toward Oregon.

Heart Mountain internment camp
Heart Mountain, Wyoming, 1943
Courtesy of S. Konno

RENEWED OPPRESSION AND FINAL STRUGGLE

Once he was our friend
The owner of the store now
Behaves nervously
Refusing to sell us goods.

Shizue Iwatsuki[106]

With the war coming to an end, Oregon experienced renewed anti-Japanese movements. In Gresham, local farmers and businessmen, inspired by the economic advantage of Japanese exclusion, started a campaign to prevent their return as early as 1943. This movement led to the establishment of the Oregon Anti-Japanese Inc., in November, 1944. Later renamed the Japanese Exclusion League, this group called for "the enactment of legislation, both State and Federal, designed to exclude from United States citizenship all persons now ineligible for citizenship, as well as their descendants."[107]

Hood River also had an exclusionist movement. As in the first organized agitation, the local American Legion took the lead. The arguments against the return of the Japanese were essentially the same as before: their low standards of living, unassimilability to American society and economic threat. The Legion published the pamphlet entitled "A Statement on the Japanese." It read:

Through the years we have seen, not the Americanization of the Japanese here, but the rapid and sure Japanization of our little valley.... The carefully organized infiltration of cohesive alien groups, the carefully organized evasion of the alien land laws, the deliberate alienation of children, and finally

*Sometimes,
I almost forget
where I am.*

Heart Mountain internment camp, softball team,
Kaoru Tsunenaga (third row, third from left)
Heart Mountain, Wyoming, ca. 1944
Courtesy of S. Tsunenaga

MINIDOKA

MINIDOKA

CONCENTRATION CAMP
U S STYLE HUNT, IDAHO

Cora and Clarence Oliver visiting interned friends at
Minidoka internment camp
Minidoka, Idaho, ca. 1943
Courtesy of M. Shiozaki

Words cannot express these feelings.

the full realization that we are faced with alternatives of abandoning our homes to an alien people or of finding lawful means to disperse these aliens.[108]

In December, 1944, the Legion removed the names of 16 Nisei servicemen, including Sgt. Frank Hachiya, from the public honor roll. This action drew a storm of criticism from the entire nation, and under the increasing pressure, the names were reinstated to the roll the following April.

However, the Hood River American Legion held to its position against Japanese

resettlement by setting up an independent organization called the Hood River Citizens Committee.[109] Between January and March, 1945, one of the Legion leaders ran full page ads in a local newspaper with the names of over 1,500 local residents who assisted "one hundred percent in *all* efforts to keep the Japs from returning to this county." With captions such as "JAPS ARE NOT WANTED IN HOOD RIVER," the ads not only publicized the doctrine of the Legion, but also attacked anyone who was supportive of Japanese resettlement.[110]

One of the few supporters of the Japanese was the local Methodist minister, Sherman Burgoyne. Assigned to the church in Hood River during the war, he had never met any of the Japanese, but, for the principles involved, he stood up for their rights and openly acted as their friend. One of the exclusionist ads called the minister a pro-Japanese and criticized him for failing to "get a true picture of the sentiment in the county."[111] The effect of the attack was so great that he faced ostracism from the white community and his wife was fired by a local bank. Reverend Burgoyne

*Each stitch,
each step on
the battlefield.*

Minidoka internment camp,
women's embroidery class
Minidoka, Idaho, ca. 1943
Courtesy of H. Saito

received the Thomas Jefferson Award from the Council Against Intolerance in 1947, and overt social intolerance began to lessen.[112]

Indeed, what awaited many Japanese Americans when they finally returned to their Oregon homes was intense antagonism. In Hood River, some of the earlier returnees were met at the station by local residents carrying anti-Japanese placards. Unable to get off the train, they had to sneak into town at night by car. Due to such extreme hostility, the WRA regularly dispatched FBI agents to protect the safety of the returnees in the valley. In

their daily lives, both the Issei and the Nisei received unfriendly, cold treatment by their old neighbors. Stores refused service to them and packing sheds did not accept their crops. The first Issei returnee recalls the days of anxiety: "[T]he town rejected us…. We were caught in the fear that somebody might come to attack us, and we jumped even at the creaking of a door or at mice running on the ceiling at night."[113]

The renewed anti-Japanese agitation discouraged many Japanese Americans from returning to Gresham and Hood River. In

comparing the 1950 statistics of the Gresham-Troutdale Japanese farmers to the 1942 figures, there was more than a forty percent drop in the Japanese farming population.[114] In Hood River, the local Japanese population before mass exclusion was 579: 184 Issei and 395 Nisei. Yet, by 1950, only 233 Japanese had returned to the Hood River Valley.[115] Masuo Yasui, former community leader, was one of those who did not return after the war, although he still retained ownership of one orchard. Based on his arrest by the FBI and four-year incarceration in various Justice

First Sergeant Tami Takemoto killed
in North Africa, June 27, 1944
Courtesy of M. Takemoto

Mother, please don't worry...

Minidoka internment camp, English class
Minidoka, Idaho, 1944
Courtesy of H. Saito

*Out there, somewhere,
is a place for me.*

Department camps, local exclusionists contended that Yasui was "a traitor, a spy, and a
dangerous enemy alien."[116] Given veiled
threats of violence from former neighbors, he
had to give up resettlement in the valley community and move to Portland where he could
still see his beloved Mt. Hood from a distance.

In the eyes of the returning internees,
Portland was the safest and most welcome
place in western Oregon. In February, 1945,
a coalition of religious leaders, educators
and civil rights activists formed the Portland
Citizens Committee and assisted the Japanese

in finding housing and getting employment
with union membership.[117] The Oregon
Congress of Industrial Organizations (CIO)
also declared its full cooperation with
Japanese resettlement and accused the exclusionists in Hood River and Gresham of
"arousing racial prejudices for their own par-
tisan ends."[118] Furthermore, under the
auspices of the Oregon Methodist Church
Conference, the Japanese Methodist Church
building was opened to those who needed
temporary shelter. Such a favorable climate
induced many people to choose Portland as

the place to start over. By 1946, a total of 463
Issei and 396 Nisei came back to the city.[119]

After the war, the Issei left community
affairs to their children, primarily because of
the devastating effects of mass internment and
their age. Upon returning to Portland, Issei
elders agreed that the local JACL should
assume community leadership, and they did
not form any central organization equivalent
to the pre-war Japanese Association. Other
communities like Gresham and Hood River
had the Issei-led Nikkeijin-kai. However, they
were, by and large, social clubs, and matters

*One kind man
makes all
the difference.*

Reverend Sherman Burgoyne
and Mrs. Suye Ogawa
discussing resettlement
Hood River, Oregon, ca. 1946
Courtesy of Oregon Historical
Society (ORHI 87184)

of community and political concerns were left in the hands of the Nisei.[120]

The notable exception was the Issei leadership in the struggle to overturn the alien land laws in the latter half of 1940s. In early 1945, the Oregon state legislature had passed the second Alien Land Law backed by the Hood River and Gresham exclusionists. The new law, a supplement to the 1923 statute, was extremely oppressive to the Issei because it even denied their right to live and work on farmlands. In addition to the ban on Japanese leasehold and land ownership, the law had a provision under which any such individual who "shall till, farm, or work land in the state or occupy the same in any capacity" is presumed as the "owner of a leasehold or some interest in land." Hence, it could be a criminal offense for the Issei to simply work on somebody's farm. Furthermore, a Nisei could be also prosecuted if it was established under the law that he/she entered a lease contract with the intention to have "aliens ineligible to citizenship" occupy or work on the land.[121] Facing the risk of making their children "criminals," the Issei even had to stay away from their children's farms.

In cooperation with the Portland JACL, the Issei fought the law. With Issei leader Daiichi Takeoka as the chairperson, they formed the Committee for the Oregon Alien Land Law Test Case in April, 1946. Learning that the Multnomah County Bar Association was critically looking into the 1945 statute from a legal standpoint, the committee decided to work with the Bar Association and hired its president Verne Dusenbery and Allan Hart as their legal counsels. One year after the establishment of the Committee, a suit was filed at

Issei becoming naturalized citizens
Hood River, Oregon, ca. 1954
Courtesy of M. Yasui

Underneath, I am the same person.

*Our son will always
be an American.*

Gold Star parents dedicating the Nisei
Memorial at Rose City Cemetery
Portland, Oregon, October 31, 1954
Courtesy of F. Nakata

the Multnomah County Circuit Court on behalf of an Issei father and Nisei son who sought to lease a farm in Gresham.[122]

For the test case, the Committee chose Etsuo Namba, an Issei who had farmed in Gresham since 1917, and Kenji Namba, a Nisei who fought in the 442nd Regimental Combat Team. In January and February of 1947, the Nambas negotiated with a landowner to lease 62 acres for five years. Although the Issei father and Nisei son had separate contracts, dividing the land in half, neither of the two leases could be executed unless the

other was also executed. The dwelling house was located in the west section of the land which Kenji was to lease. Under this arrangement, as the plaintiffs expected, the court was required to rule on both the Issei's right to lease land and the constitutionality of the 1945 statute which prohibited the Issei from living with the Nisei on a leasehold.[123]

The court case continued for two years. In October, 1947, the Multnomah County Circuit Court fundamentally upheld the ban on leasehold by the Issei.[124] The Japanese appealed the decision and brought their case

before the Oregon State Supreme Court. March 29, 1949, the Court reversed the previous decision and ruled that the laws violated the equal protection clause of the Fourteenth Amendment. The judge argued:

The several hundred alien Japanese to whom the Alien Land Law is applicable came to our state lawfully under laws enacted by Congress. They are here lawfully and are entitled to remain. Many of them are parents of United States citizens, and some of them are mothers and fathers of American soldiers who gave a good account

Greetings from the Oregon Issei Pioneers and friends, Portland, Oregon, May 6, 1993, photographer, Greg Kozawa

Fellowship, community –
"in this great land
of freedom."

of themselves in the recent war. Our country cannot afford to create, by legislation or judicial construction, a ghetto for our ineligible aliens. And yet if we deny to the alien who is lawfully here the normal means whereby he earns his livelihood, we thereby assign him to a lowered standard of living.[125]

This historic ruling not only voided the laws that had beset the Issei for many years, but also exemplified a significant change in Oregon. From exclusion to acceptance, the attitude of the dominant society was undergoing a dramatic transformation. Three years

later, America repealed the legal status of the Issei as "aliens ineligible to citizenship." The Walter-McCarran Act of 1952 allowed Japanese immigrants to become naturalized citizens of the United States, ending the long history of legal discrimination. Without question, the Issei had been "Americans" by their deeds and in their hearts, but their adopted country finally accepted them by including them in its founding principles of justice and equality. In a practical sense, it was much too late, for many Issei had already passed away and others were too old to start over. Never-

theless, it symbolically validated Issei life and their contributions to "this great land of freedom."

Pounding rice cakes to celebrate
My American citizenship
Now I am so old.

Oba Sakyu[126]

Eiichiro Azuma
Curator
Japanese American National Museum

ENDNOTES

1. To date, there are a few existing studies of the Oregon Issei: Marvin G. Pursinger, "Oregon's Japanese in World War II, A History of Compulsory Relocation," Ph.D Dissertation, University of Southern California, 1961; and "The Japanese Settle in Oregon: 1880-1920," *Journal of the West* 5:2 (April, 1966): 251-263; Marjorie R. Stearns, "The History of the Japanese People in Oregon," MA Thesis, University of Oregon, 1938; "The Settlement of the Japanese in Oregon," *Oregon Historical Quarterly* 39:3 (September, 1938): 262-269; and Barbara Yasui, "The Nikkei in Oregon, 1834-1940," *Oregon Historical Quarterly* 76:3 (September, 1975): 225-257. With an exception of Barbara Yasui, these authors rely almost exclusively on the English sources recorded by white Americans. As a result, they focus on anti-Japanese exclusionists rather than on Japanese immigrants.

2. Kazuo Ito, *Issei: A History of Japanese Immigrants in North America,* translated by Shinichiro Nakamura and Jean S. Gerard, (Seattle: Japanese Community Service, 1973), p. 29.

3. Zaibei Nihonjinkai, *Zaibei Nihonjinshi* (San Francisco: Zaibei Nihonjinkai, 1940), pp. 999-1000; Barbara Yasui, "The Nikkei in Oregon, 1834-1940," p. 228; and Marvin G. Pursinger, "The Japanese Settle in Oregon: 1880-1920," p. 251-252.

4. Gaimusho, *Nihon Gaiko Bunsho,* Vol. 24 (Tokyo: Gaimusho, 1952), pp. 495-498; and Frank M. Tomori, *Taigan no Koe* (Okayama: Tomori Yasuro, 1969), p. 60.

5. Shiro Fujioka, *Ayumi no Ato* (Los Angeles: Ayumi no Ato Kanko Koenkai, 1957), p. 352.

6. Ibid., p. 349. For more details of Tadashichi Tanaka, consult Yuji Ichioka, *The Issei: The World of the First Generation Japanese Immigrants, 1885-1924* (New York: Free Press, 1988), pp. 49-50.

7. Gaimusho, *Imin Chosa Hokoku,* Vol. 9 (Tokyo: Yushodo, 1986), pp. 40, 78.

8. Ibid., pp. 41-42; and Kazuo Ito, *Issei: A History of Japanese Immigrants in North America,* p. 313. Tally made by the author.

9. Ban contracted with the Southern Pacific, the Oregon Short Line, the Oregon Railway and Navigation Company, the Astoria and Columbia River Railway, the Chicago, Burlington and Quincy, and the Santa Fe Railroad.

10. Ofu Inshi, *Zaibei Seiko no Nihonjin* (Tokyo: Hobunkan, 1904), pp. 136-156; Jushiro Kato, *Zaibei Doho Hattenshi* (Tokyo: Hakubunkan, 1908), pp. 187-188; Junichi Torai, *Hokubei Nihonjin Soran* (Tokyo: Chuodo Shobo, 1914), pp. 123-124; *Ikkai Kashiwamura, Hokubei Tosa Taikan* (Tokyo: Ryubundo, 1911), pp. 226, 232-237.

11. Gaimusho, *Nihon Gaiko Bunsho,* Vol. 24, p. 498.

12. Gaimusho, *Imin Chosa Hokoku,* Vol. 9, pp. 116-117.

13. U.S. Department of the Interior, Census Office, *Compendium of the Eleventh Census of the U.S. 1890; Census Reports of the Twelfth Census of the U.S. 1900;* and *Thirteenth Census of the U.S.: 1910* (Washington D.C.: Government Printing Office, 1892, 1902, and 1913).

14. Tachibana Ginsha, *Hokubei Haikushu* (Los Angeles, Tachibana Ginsha, 1974), p. 37.

15. Letter from Masuo Yasui to T. Yasui, December 11, 1907, in Homer Yasui Personal Collection.

16. Kazuo Ito, *Issei: A History of Japanese Immigrants in North America,* p. 344.

17. Ibid., pp. 291-302.

18. Gaimusho, *Nihon Gaiko Bunsho,* Vol. 24, pp. 498-499.

19. Gaimusho, *Nihon Gaiko Bunsho: Taibei Imin Mondai Keika Gaiyo* (Tokyo: Gaimusho, 1972), pp. 198-199.

20. Kazuo Ito, *Issei: A History of Japanese Immigrants in North America,* p. 766.

21. The founding members of the church were Shinzaburo Ban and Shintaro Takaki.

22. Buddhist Churches of America, *Buddhist Churches of America: 75 Year History, 1899-1974* (Chicago: Buddhist Churches of America, 1974), pp. 182-186.

23. Tachibana Ginsha, *Hokubei Haikushu,* p. 37.

24. Gaimusho, *Nihon Gaiko Bunsho: Taibei Imin Mondai Keika Gaiyo,* p. 375.

25. Nichibei Shimbun-sha, *Nichibei Nenkan,* Vol. 6 (San Francisco: Nichibei Shimbun-sha, 1910), pp. 203-204.

26. Ibid., p. 203.

27. Marjorie R. Stearns, "The History of the Japanese People in Oregon," p. 2. In her thesis, she calls the community "Russellville" instead of "Montavilla." However, the common name that Japanese immigrants usually used to refer to the community was Montavilla.

28. Junichi Torai, *Hokubei Nihonjin Soran,* pp. 126-133.

29. Frank Davey, *Report on the Japanese Situation in Oregon* (Salem: State Printing Department, 1920), p. 5.

30. Nichibei Shimbun-sha, *Nichibei Nenkan,* Vol. 6, p. 204.

31. Hokubei Jiji-sha, *Hokubei Nenkan,* Vol. 2 (Seattle: Hokubei Jiji-sha, 1911), p. 228; and Nichibei Shimbun-sha, *Nichibei Nenkan,* Vol. 10 (San Francisco: Nichibei Shimbun-sha, 1914), pp. 158-159.

32. Frank Davey, *Report on the Japanese Situation in Oregon,* p. 14; Barbara Yasui, "The Nikkei in Oregon, 1834-1940," pp. 241-242.

33. Letter from Masuo Yasui to Renichi Fujimoto, June 14, 1907, in Homer Yasui Collection. The ideal of permanent settlement was shared with other prominent Issei leaders. In California, for example, Kyutaro Abiko disseminated the ideal through his newspaper, the *Nichibei Shimbun.* In order to put it into practice, he also purchased a large tract in the central San Joaquin Valley, which he subdivided into smaller parcels for the Issei who intended to settle down as farmers. Before moving to Hood River, Masuo Yasui apparently had studied Abiko's project as a model.

34. Robert Yasui, *The Yasui Family of Hood River, Oregon* (Hood River, OR: Holly Yasui, 1987), pp. 6, 10; and Barbara Yasui, "The Nikkei in Oregon, 1834-1940," p. 241.

35. Robert Yasui, *The Yasui Family of Hood River, Oregon,* pp. 7-8; Barbara Yasui, "The Nikkei in Oregon, 1834-1940," pp. 248-249.

36. Hokubei Jiji-sha, *Hokubei Nenkan* (Seattle: Hokubei Jiji-sha, 1936), pp. 207, 222.

37. Marvin G. Pursinger, "The Japanese Settle in Oregon, 1880-1920," p. 257; Kojiro Takeuchi, *Beikoku Seihokubu Nihon Iminshi,* (Seattle: Taihoku Nippo, 1929), p. 885; and Kazuo Ito, *Issei: A History of Japanese Immigrants in North America,* pp. 513-514.

38. Letter from Roy Fukuda to Chas. L. McNary, October 2, 1925, in Frank Fukuda Personal Collection.

39. Letter from Chas. L. McNary to Roy Fukuda, November 2, 1925, in Frank Fukuda Personal Collection.

40. Ko Murai, *Zaibei Nihonjin Sangyo Soran* (Los Angeles: Beikoku Sangyo Nippo-sha, 1940), pp. 963-964.

41. Letter from Masuo Yasui to Renichi Fujimoto, April 1, 1907, in Homer Yasui Personal Collection.

42. Many Japanese immigrant males married women in Japan whom they had not known except through the exchange of their photos. Since marriage in Japan only required the transfer of a wife's name into the husband's family register, or vice versa, such a practice was perfectly legal.

43. U.S. Bureau of the Census, *Fourteenth Census of the United States: 1920;* and *Fifteenth Census of the United States: 1930* (Washington D.C.: Government Printing Office, 1922 and 1933).

44. Kazuo Ito, *Issei: A History of Japanese Immigrants in North America,* p. 499.

45. Ibid., pp. 500-501.

46. Ibid., p. 501.

47. Zaibei Nihonjinkai, *Zaibei Nihonjinshi,* pp. 1005-1006.

48. Ibid., p. 1005. The farmers associations include the Oregon Cauliflower Growers Association, the Portland Cauliflower Growers Association, the Oregon Pea Growers Association, the Oregon Celery Growers Association, and the Oregon Strawberry Growers Association. Some of these had their own cold storage and packing facilities.

49. Marvin G. Pursinger, "Oregon's Japanese in World War II, A History of Compulsory Relocation," p. 64.

50. In Oregon, there were local Japanese associations or equivalents in the communities of Montavilla, Gresham-Troutdale, Columbia Boulevard, Sherwood, Banks, Clackamas, Dee, Hood River, The Dalles, Baker, Independence and Medford.

51. Zaibei Nihonjinkai, *Zaibei Nihonjinshi,* pp. 1002-1003.

52. Ikkai Kashiwamura, *Hokubei Tosa Taikan,* p. 231; and Zaibei Nihonjinkai, *Zaibei Nihonjinshi,* p. 1003.

53. Tachibana Ginsha, *Hokubei Haikushu,* p. 37.

54. Marjorie R. Stearns, "The History of the Japanese People in Oregon," pp. 6-9; and Barbara Yasui, "The Nikkei in Oregon, 1834-1940," pp. 242-244.

55. The 1920 U.S. Census showed the existence of 351 Japanese in Hood River, while the Japanese Consulate statistics indicated 389 Japanese.

56. Barbara Yasui, "The Nikkei in Oregon, 1834-1940," p. 243; and Marjorie R. Stearns, "The History of the Japanese People in Oregon," pp. 8, 22-23, 25, 27-28.

57. Masuo Yasui, "Request to Japanese Ladies," ca. 1920, in Yasui Brothers Manuscript Collection, the Oregon Historical Society (hereafter, OHS).

58. *Hood River News,* January 16, 1920; and Letter from the Anti-Asiatic Association to M. Yasui, January 31, 1920, in Yasui Brothers Manuscript Collection, OHS.

59. Marjorie R. Stearns, "The History of the Japanese People in Oregon," pp. 25-26.

60. Ibid., p. 9.

61. Ibid., pp. 9-13.

62. The alien land bills of 1917 and 1919 did not prohibit Japanese leasehold, but limited it to the maximum of three years.

63. Letter from Senichi Tomihiro to Masuo Yasui, January 30, 1917, in Yasui Brothers Manuscript Collection, OHS. Also see Marjorie R. Stearns, "The History of the Japanese People in Oregon," pp. 45 and 57.

64. Letter from Senichi Tomihiro to Masuo Yasui, February 14, 1917, in Yasui Brothers Manuscript Collection, OHS.

65. For more details of the Takao Ozawa case, see Yuji Ichioka, *The Issei: The World of the First Generation Japanese Immigrants, 1885-1924* (New York: Free Press, 1988), pp. 210-226.

66. Kojiro Takeuchi, *Beikoku Seihokubu Nihon Iminshi,* pp. 675-677; *Taihoku Nippo,* February 26, 1923.

67. *Taihoku Nippo,* July 24, 1926; Kojiro Takeuchi, *Beikoku Seihokubu Nihon Iminshi,* pp. 671-673. See also Stefan Tanaka, "The Toledo Incident: The Deportation of the Nikkei from an Oregon Mill Town," *Pacific Northwest Quarterly* 69:3 (July, 1978), 116-126.

68. Eliot G. Mears, *Residential Orientals on the American Pacific Coast: Their Legal and Economic Status* (Chicago: The University of Chicago Press, 1928), pp. 420-421; and Oregon Bureau of Labor, Census: *Japanese Population in Oregon* (Salem: State Printing Department, 1929). Tally by the author.

69. *Taihoku Nippo,* May 14, 1923.

70. Marvin G. Pursinger, "Oregon's Japanese in World War II, A History of Compulsory Relocation," pp. 430-436.

71. Ibid., p. 46.